SURVIVING WITH DOPAMINE:

Understanding dopamine and how it affects our daily lifestyle.

Stephen M.White

TABLE OF CONTENT

CHAPTER 1

CHAPTER 2

CHAPTER 3

CHAPTER 4

CHAPTER 5

CHAPTER 6

CHAPTER 7

CHAPTER 8

CHAPTER 1

Introduction

Dopamine is considered the brain's "feel good" chemical messenger; it motivates us to seek out rewards such as food, sex, and social engagement. Historically, researchers assumed that dopamine was subconsciously released when the brain expects a reward. Furthermore, they thought that this mechanism enabled neurons in the brain to communicate and control movement in response to the anticipated reward (Marsden, 2006). This finding contradicts the longstanding perception of the function of neurotransmitters and provides evidence that our brains can learn to control seemingly subconscious neurological processes.Dopamine (DA) has been one of the most extensively researched neurotransmitters in the brain in the 50 years after its discovery.Dopaminergic systems have been examined from the viewpoints of cognitive development and aging, as well as in relation to neuropsychiatric and other diseases (such as schizophrenia, attention deficit hyperactivity disorder (ADHD), Parkinson's disease [PD], and drug addiction). This widespread interest in DA is largely due to the diverse variety of motor control, motivational, and cognitive tasks that engage these networks, as well as DA's significant neuromodulatory role in several subcortical and cortical neural networks.

It should come as no surprise that brain DA levels have an impact on how many distinct behaviors are carried out.

Is mediating that behavior, the neural underpinnings of that system, the DA projections into the pertinent brain regions, and the time course of DA release in those regions in order to make accurate predictions about how DA-related medications will affect a behavior.

The neocortex is the part of the cerebral cortex that consists of gray matter and is where higher cognitive functioning originates from. In mice, the neocortex is flooded with unpredictable dopamine impulses at a rate of about 0.01 times per second.

This research is groundbreaking in establishing a new connection between dopamine and the salience of rewards. The ability to potentially control our response to rewards through intentional manipulation of dopamine impulses has vast implications and prompts further research into the exact mechanism of neurotransmitters in the brain.Neurotransmitters are substances produced by neurons. Through the transmission of "signals" to carry out certain bodily activities, these chemical messengers connect the brain and spinal cord to muscles, organs, and glands. In order to control emotions, memory, cognitive function, attention span, energy, hunger, cravings, susceptibility to pain, and sleep patterns, they also interact with particular areas in the brain known as receptors.

These chemical imbalances affect our behavior and quality of life and can lead to a variety of health problems.

Dopamine is believed to play a role in many important functions in your body, mainly those that deal with mental function, emotional response, and physical reactions.

These include

Behaviors involving motivation, punishment, and reward
Cognitive functions involving attention, learning, and working (short-term) memory
Voluntary movement
Pain processing
Sleep and dreaming
Mood regulation
While it's colloquially known as the chemical that makes you happy, it primarily does this in ways that involve reward and motivation.

For example, when you taste your favorite ice cream, you get a dopamine boost and it makes you happy, which gives you the motivation to have another taste. Even anticipating a reward can increase the amount of dopamine activity in your brain.

Dopamine is one of the better-known brain chemicals, with lots of attention for its role as a "happy" chemical or relating to addiction. It has numerous important roles beyond that, though, and plays a big part in a host of medical conditions including addiction, schizophrenia, and Parkinson's disease.

As researchers have uncovered more about brain chemistry and function in general, and about how specific chemicals work, their understanding of this key chemical has grown by leaps and bounds. That means the diagnosis and treatment of dopamine-related conditions are getting better all the time.Dihydroxyphenylalanine (dopa), an intermediate product generated during the metabolism of the amino acid tyrosine, is the source of dopamine, also known as hydroxytyramine, an organic compound that contains nitrogen. The hormones norepinephrine and epinephrine are precursors to it. The substantia nigra, basal ganglia, and corpus striatum of the brain also operate as dopamine neurotransmitters, chiefly by slowing the passage of nerve impulses.

What Is Dopamine?

So is dopamine your cupcake addiction? Your gambling? Your alcoholism? Your sex life? The reality is dopamine has something to do with all of these. But it is none of them. Dopamine is a chemical in your body. That's all. But that doesn't make it simple.

What is dopamine? Dopamine is one of the chemical signals that pass information from one neuron to the next in the tiny spaces between them. When it is released from the first neuron, it floats into the space (the synapse) between the two neurons, and it bumps against receptors on the other side that then send a signal down the receiving neuron. That sounds very simple, but when you scale it up from a single pair of neurons to the vast networks in your brain, it quickly becomes complex. The effects of dopamine release depend on where it's coming from, where the receiving neurons are going and what type of neurons they are, what receptors are binding the dopamine (there are five known types), and what role both the releasing and receiving neurons are playing.

Brain chemicals like dopamine are called neurotransmitters. The word describes their function—they transmit chemical messages between neurons (brain and nerve cells). Outside of your brain, dopamine is a hormone.

Each neurotransmitter has a variety of functions and impacts multiple areas of the brain. They have different jobs in different regions. For example, in the movement centers of the brain, dopamine deals with movement. In the learning areas, though, it deals with attention.

To transmit messages through your nervous system, a neurotransmitter binds to a receptor that's specifically made for it. It's like a key slipping into a lock. Dopamine can only interact with neurons that have dopamine receptors.

When a neurotransmitter's functioning is impaired, it leads to symptoms that are associated with its normal roles. This is called neurotransmitter dysregulation.

You may hear or read about "low levels" or "high levels" of dopamine and other neurotransmitters, but in many cases, experts aren't sure whether symptoms are caused by:

Abnormal levels, with producing too much or too little of the neurotransmitter
Abnormal receptor sensitivity, meaning that the "locks" on neurons aren't responding properly to dopamine as "key"
Too few receptors, meaning dopamine can interact with fewer neurons
Too many receptors, meaning dopamine can interact with more neurons

According to a study published in 2020, the areas of the brain most affected by dopamine appear to be the motor cortex and the insular cortex (also called the insula), but it has widespread influence.

The motor cortex deals with movement. The insular cortex is important for homeostasis, which is how your body maintains a proper temperature, signals that you're hungry, regulates heartbeat and breathing, and generally keeps things running within proper parameters.

Anatomy of the Brain
Relationship to Norepinephrine
Dopamine has a close relationship with the neurotransmitter norepinephrine. Your body makes norepinephrine and dopamine from some of the same chemicals, they appear to bind to some of the same receptors, and they work together to perform many functions.

If addiction is a sickness or a choice, and whether low dopamine levels may be a contributing factor, are hot topics in today's medical world. Certain experts in the field of addiction medicine contend that some people are more genetically prone to addiction than others, arguing that a person's DNA determines how likely they are to develop an addiction. Each person reacts differently to chemicals. For instance, some people get drunk relatively quickly, while others may consume more alcohol before being intoxicated. Variations in a person's genetic composition may have an impact on differences like these.

The "genetic predisposition to addiction" theory's main defense centers on genetic variations connected to these kinds of reactions. According to this notion, there may be an underlying genetic component that contributes to substance abuse running in families.

According to scientists, hereditary factors may be to blame for roughly 50% of our susceptibility to addiction. Technology has allowed scientists to identify certain gene sequences that appear to be associated with a higher risk of drug or alcohol addiction. These gene sequences control how specific proteins are made by the body. Our chances of being addicted can be affected by how these proteins function or don't function.

For instance, a research found that mice with reduced PSD-95 levels had increased sensitivity to cocaine. PSD-95-normal mice had a lower chance of developing cocaine addiction. Another animal research found that the brain is affected and influenced by cocaine, opioids, and amphetamines using a protein called DARPP-32. Mice who had previously misused medications stopped reacting to them after the protein was taken out of the brain. Research has shown that genetics can also raise the chance of addiction in people, despite the fact that these studies were conducted on mice.

According to scientific evidence, a kid of an addict has an 8-fold increased risk of being addicted. Generational addiction is more frequent than most people know since most families don't discuss their history of drug use. Knowing your family's history of addiction is crucial since an estimated 80 million Americans presently live with or have previously lived with a spouse or family member who is battling with alcoholism.

Although addiction is a complicated disorder that isn't brought on by a single reason, scientists do think that our DNA may really be able to influence whether we get addicted or not.

"This [relationship] isn't always a gene for a certain feature. It's a connection between genes and the environment, Dr. Kathleen Brady said. You might have a genetic predisposition for substance use disorders but not really acquire one if you live in a protected environment, she said. "However, there may be epigenetic alterations that cause you to have an increased stress response to future stress and be more susceptible to the development of alcohol dependency if you have the gene for alcohol consumption and you encounter some kind of early life trauma."

In other words, our genes dictate how we react to adversity, which might influence whether we abuse addictive substances or not. The good news is that we are not defined by our DNA. Despite our genetic make-up, we may prevent and terminate the cycle of addiction by learning healthy coping mechanisms, recovering from prior trauma, and spending time in wholesome, secure situations.

CHAPTER 2

What Dopamine Does Daily

Dopamine is believed to play a role in many important functions in your body, mainly those that deal with mental function, emotional response, and physical reactions.

These include

Behaviors involving motivation, punishment, and reward
Cognitive functions involving attention, learning, and working (short-term) memory
Voluntary movement
Pain processing

Sleep and dreaming
Mood regulation
While it's colloquially known as the chemical that makes you happy, it primarily does this in ways that involve reward and motivation.

In an unprecedented attack of candor, Sean Parker, the 38-year-old founding president of Facebook, admitted that the social network was founded not to unite us, but to distract us. "The thought process was: 'How do we consume as much of your time and conscious attention as possible?'" he said at an event in Philadelphia in November. To achieve this goal, Facebook's architects exploited a "vulnerability in human psychology", explained Parker, who resigned from the company in 2005. Whenever someone likes or comments on a post or photograph, he said, "we… give you a little dopamine hit". Facebook is an empire of empires, then, built upon a molecule.

Dopamine, discovered in 1957, is one of 20 or so major neurotransmitters, a flect of chemicals that, like bicycle couriers weaving through traffic, carry urgent messages between neurons, nerves and other cells in the body. These neurotransmitters ensure our hearts keep beating, our lungs keep breathing and, in dopamine's case, that we know to get a glass of water when we feel thirsty, or attempt to procreate so that our genes may survive our death.

In the 1950s, dopamine was thought to be largely associated with physical movement after a study showed that Parkinsonism (a group of neurological disorders whose symptoms include tremors, slow movement and stiffness) was caused by dopamine deficiency. In the 1980s, that assumption changed following a series of experiments on rats by Wolfram Schultz, now a professor of neuroscience at Cambridge University, which showed that, inside the midbrain, dopamine relates to the reward we receive for an action. Dopamine, it seemed, was to do with desire, ambition, addiction and sex drive.

Schultz and his fellow researchers placed pieces of apple behind a screen and immediately saw a major dopamine response when the rat bit into the food. This dopamine process, which is common in all insects and mammals, is, Schultz tells me, at the basis of learning: it anticipates a reward to an action and, if the reward is met, enables the behavior to become a habit, or, if there's a discrepancy, to be adapted. (That dishwasher tablet might look like a delicious sweet, but the first fizzing bite will also be the last.) Whether dopamine produces a pleasurable sensation is unclear, says Schultz. But this has not dented its reputation as the miracle bestower of happiness.

We are abusing a useful and necessary system. We shouldn't do it, even though we can

Dopamine inspires us to take actions to meet our needs and desires – anything from turning up the heating to satisfying a craving to spin a roulette wheel – by anticipating how we will feel after they're met.

"We found a signal in the brain that explains our most profound behaviors, in which every one of us is engaged constantly," says Shultz. "I can see why the public has become interested."

In this way, unlike its obscure co-workers norepinephrine and asparagine, dopamine has become a celebrity molecule. The British clinical psychologist Vaughan Bell once described dopamine as "the Kim Kardashian of molecules". In the tabloid press, dopamine has become the transmitter for hyperbole. "Are cupcakes as addictive as cocaine?" ran one headline in the Sun, citing a study that showed dopamine was released in the orbital frontal cortex – "the same section activated when cocaine addicts are shown a bag of the class A drug" – when participants were shown pictures of their favorite foods. Still, nowhere is dopamine more routinely name-dropped than in Silicon Valley, where it is hailed as the secret sauce that makes an app, game or social platform "sticky" – the investor term for "potentially profitable".

"Even a year or two before the scene about persuasive tech grew up, dopamine was a molecule that had a certain edge and sexiness to it in the cultural zeitgeist," explains Ramsay Brown, the 28-year-old cofounder of Dopamine Labs, a controversial California startup that promises to significantly increase the rate at which people use any running, diet or game app. "It is the sex, drugs and rock'n'roll molecule. While there are many important and fascinating questions that sit at the base of this molecule, when you say 'dopamine', people's ears prick up in a way they don't when you say 'enkephalin' or 'glutamate'. It's the known fun transmitter."

Fun, perhaps, but as with Kardashian, dopamine's press is not entirely favorable. In a 2017 article titled "How evil is tech?", the New York Times columnist David Brooks wrote: "Tech companies understand what causes dopamine surges in the brain and they lace their products with 'hijacking techniques' that lure us in and create 'compulsion loops'." Most social media sites create irregularly timed rewards, Brooks wrote, a technique long employed by the makers of slot machines, based on the work of the American psychologist BF Skinner, who found that the strongest way to reinforce a learned behavior in rats is to reward it on a random schedule. "When a gambler feels favored by luck, dopamine is released," says Natasha Schüll, a professor at New York University and author of Addiction By Design: Machine Gambling in Las Vegas. This is the secret to Facebook's era-defining success: we compulsively check the site because we never know when the delicious ting of social affirmation may sound.

Randomness is at the heart of Dopamine Labs' service, a system that can be implemented into any app designed to build habitual behavior. In a running app, for example, this means only issuing encouragement – a high-five badge, or a shower of digital confetti – at random intervals, rather than every time the user completes a run. "When you finish a run, the app communicates with our system and asks whether it would be surprising to him if we congratulated him a little more enthusiastically," explains Brown. Dopamine Labs' proprietary AI uses machine learning to tailor the schedule of rewards to an individual. "It might say: actually, right now he'd see it coming, so don't give it to him now. Or it might say: GO!"

While the sale seems preposterously flimsy (with a slot machine, for example, at least the random reward is money, a much more compelling prize than any digital badge), Brown says that the running app company has seen significant positive results. "If you do this properly, we see an average 30% improvement in the frequency of how often a person goes for a run." Dopamine Labs, which currently has 10 clients, has seen similar positive results with many other kinds of apps. In one dieting service, which encourages people to track the food they eat, the company saw an 11% increase in food-tracking after integrating Dopamine Labs' system. A microloan service saw a 14% improvement in how frequently people would pay back their loans on time or early. "An anti-cyberbullying app saw a 167% improvement in how often young people sent encouraging messages to one another by controlling when and how often and when we sent them an animated gif reward," claims Brown.

The capacity for so-called "persuasive technology" to influence behavior in this way is only just becoming understood, but the power of the dopamine system to alter habits is already familiar to drug addicts and smokers. Every habit-forming drug, from amphetamines to cocaine, from nicotine to alcohol, affects the dopamine system by dispersing many times more dopamine than usual. The use of these drugs overruns the neural pathways connecting the reward circuit to the prefrontal cortex, which helps people to tame impulses. The more an addict uses a drug, the harder it becomes to stop.

"These unnaturally large rewards are not filtered in the brain – they go directly into the brain and overstimulate, which can generate addiction," explains Shultz. "When that happens, we lose our willpower. Evolution has not prepared our brains for these drugs, so they become overwhelmed and screwed up. We are abusing a useful and necessary system. We shouldn't do it, even though we can." Dopamine's power to negatively affect a life can be seen vividly in the effects of some Parkinson's drugs, which, in flooding the brain with dopamine, have been shown to turn close to 10% of patients into gambling addicts.

A Neuroscientist Explains: season two trailer – podcast
Brown and his colleagues are aware that they're playing with fire and claim to have developed a robust ethical framework for the kinds of companies and app-makers with which they will work. "We spend time with them, understand what they're building and why," he says. "The ethics test looks something like: should this work in this app? Should this change human behaviors? Does this app encourage human flourishing? If not, does it at least not make the human condition shittier?" To date, Brown claims that Dopamine Labs has

turned down both betting companies and free-to-play video game developers, who wanted to use the company's services to form habits in their players.

Well-intentioned strategies often produce unintended consequences. "I don't know whether [these apps] can generate addiction," says Schultz, who, along with two other researchers, was awarded Denmark's €1m Brain prize in 2017 for discovering dopamine's effects. "But the idea behind behavioral economics, that we can change the behavior of others not via drugs or hitting them on the head, but by putting them into particular situations, is controversial. We are telling other people what is good for them, which carries risks. Training people via systems to release dopamine for certain actions could even cause situations where people can't then get away from the system. I'm not saying technology companies are doing bad things.

They may be helping. But I would be careful."

For Brown, however, co-opting these systems to produce positive effects is the safest and most logical way in which to evolve the human mind, and use a natural molecule to form intentional, positive habits. "We can close the gap between aspiration and behavior and build systems that enrich the human condition and encourage human flourishing," he says. "Our product is a slot machine that plays you."The brain is a complicated organ that assists us in carrying out everyday duties and ultimately achieving long-term professional objectives. But the same organ may also easily lead us astray, particularly in an age when the internet is so readily accessible for diversions.

We may be concentrating on our job one moment and then find ourselves giggling at a kitten video or leaving a social media remark the next.

To keep my thoughts on track, I sometimes feel like I must treat myself like a lab rat. To remain awake, I employ the Pomodoro Technique, which involves working for 25 minutes and then pausing for 5 minutes.

I set aside time each day for checking emails. I arrange my neighborhood strolls. I continue to burn out or waste time on YouTube or chat, for some reason. I'm a perpetual scientific experiment.

Dopamine is to blame, according to mental health professionals. Whether we're binge-watching the most recent Stranger Things season or obsessively checking messages or emails, it happens at work. Our bodies are trained to seek more of the things we appreciate.

Here are some particular suggestions for gaining greater control of your everyday activities, as well as the science underlying dopamine.

One of the most significant brain chemicals, dopamine is responsible for many of the actions that set humans apart from other animals. Although it controls concentration and other cognitive processes, its function also controls pleasure.

Dopamine is produced when you have a pleasurable experience, making you want to repeat that action. If such pleasure is obtained by the use of substances like alcohol, drugs, or yes, even technology, it may ultimately result in addiction and other problems.

The reaction that forces you to ignore your schedule and check your phone each time it beeps at you might lead to issues. This addiction could prevent you from having a productive workday, which will ultimately hinder your ability to advance in your profession.

Aside from destroying your productivity, succumbing to the effects of dopamine may also be detrimental to your general mental health. This is particularly true if you often use Facebook to obtain a dopamine rush since research shows that excessive usage may be detrimental to your self-esteem and overall well being. Additionally, it might result in multitasking, which hinders your ability to finish the activities you set out to achieve.

One research indicated that binge viewing hours of TV causes a decline in both comprehension and retention, so you could be doing yourself a harm when you engage in such behavior. You're not

Understanding why your actions are occurring is the first step in taking control of them. Every time your phone dings, you feel the desire to check it out as a pleasure-reward reaction. By seeing it in that light, you may be able to maintain your attention more on the task at hand and, at the very least, temporarily disable audible pings.

The time limiting for emails and other tasks is another option. Some of the smartest people do this. However, what happens if that new client who has the potential to be very profitable sends you a chat or if your highest-paying client phones you in the midst of "e-mail time"?

What if the person you've been dying to go on a date with texts you?

Uh, oh. I just received notice that the new Avengers movie's trailer had been released. Work suddenly goes by the wayside, and I find myself surrounded by distractions.

First and foremost, remember that you are just human. Maintain your course while allowing yourself to address more urgent matters when they come up. Once you take a break, meditate (or do nothing at all for a change). Balance is the key.

The greatest solution, though, could be for you (and me) to embrace waiting as a necessary aspect of life. There's something to be said about the exhilaration of anticipating the start of a trip or just waiting until tonight to see the Avengers teaser.

You'll be able to keep your days busy with hard work and actually appreciate the tiny joys in life, a little at a time, if you can find a way to postpone satisfaction a little.

CHAPTER 3

Low Dopamine

Low dopamine activity can have different physical, cognitive (thinking), and emotional effects. The symptoms of the different conditions vary, depending on the region of the brain where dopamine activity is lacking.

Symptoms of inadequate dopamine activity include:

Rigid muscles that feel stiff and achy
Tremors
Muscle
cramps or spasms
Diminished balance and coordination

A characteristic gait (walking pattern), often involving small, shuffling steps
Impairment of fine motor skills (like holding a pencil or threading a needle)
Constipation
Difficulty eating and swallowing
Cognitive impairment ("brain fog")
Difficulties with focusing attention
Fatigue
Lack of energy
Slow movement or speech
Mood swings
Low sex drive
Depression
Problems with motivation or concentration
Working memory issues, such as difficulty remembering the first part of a sentence a person just spoke
Restless leg syndrome
Shaking hands or other tremors
Changes in coordination
Inability to feel pleasure from previously enjoyed activities

Symptoms of attention-deficit hyperactivity (ADHD)

If you've experienced several of these symptoms together, you may not have even realized they could all be related. Be sure to bring up all of your symptoms to your healthcare provider so you can be properly diagnosed and treated.
Why Do Dopamine Levels Drop?
Low dopamine levels might result from a variety of factors. Some of them consist of:

Low dopamine levels have been connected to a number of medical disorders. Low dopamine levels are frequently caused by illnesses including schizophrenia, Parkinson's disease, depression, substance addiction, and bipolar disorder.
Deficient dopamine levels may result from a poor diet, especially one low in tyrosine, which is a vitamin necessary for proper brain function.

Abuse of drugs and alcohol: Over time, abusing these substances might lead your body to produce less dopamine naturally. You then start to depend on the drug you are misusing as a result of this.Dopamine deficiency is linked to numerous ailments, including Parkinson's, schizophrenia, and addiction.

Dopamine is manufactured in the midbrain, in two separate regions called the tegmental area and substantia nigra. Damage to these brain regions may affect dopamine production. A person may also experience symptoms of low dopamine when their body does not properly respond to dopamine. Drugs that inhibit the reuptake of dopamine allow the brain to access more dopamine, potentially reversing some forms of dopamine deficiency.

Bupropion, a noradrenaline and dopamine reuptake inhibitor, increases dopamine levels in the brain. It is a popular smoking cessation treatment that doctors also prescribe to treat depression and seasonal affective disorder (SAD).

Dopamine is listed on the World Health Organization's List of Essential Medicines. It can treat several life-threatening conditions, including dangerously low blood pressure and cardiac arrest, especially in newborns.

SIGNS OF LOW DOPAMINE

Dopamine affects many brain functions and physical symptoms, so signs of low dopamine may vary greatly. Some of them include:

Depression
Problems with motivation or concentration
Working memory issues, such as difficulty remembering the first part of a sentence a person just spoke.

Symptoms of schizophrenia, such as hearing voices or believing things that cannot be true

Symptoms of dementia, such as problems with executive functioning, short-term memory, managing daily tasks, or solving simple cognitive problems

Depending on the brain systems affected, a person's lifestyle, genetics, and myriad other factors, low dopamine may manifest much differently from person to person. For example, addiction, depression, and dementia are all linked to low dopamine.

Age, health status, brain injuries, and chronic medical conditions can change dopamine levels. So a person who has normal dopamine at one point in their life may still later be affected by dopamine-related health issues.

Low dopamine is not a medical diagnosis, and doctors rarely check dopamine levels. To treat low dopamine, doctors first look at symptoms, then assess a person to determine the right diagnosis. Treatment is based on the specific condition a person has. Even when a person has low dopamine, increasing dopamine levels is not always the right treatment. People with Parkinson's disease may take a form of dopamine to help with movement disorders, while those with depression may use antidepressants that target serotonin.

DOPAMINE AND MENTAL HEALTH ISSUES

Numerous mental and neurological health conditions are linked to dopamine issues. Drugs and alcohol temporarily flood the brain with dopamine. The pleasurable sensations this causes can encourage a person to continue seeking out addictive substances. Over time, however, the person needs more and more of the addictive substance to get the same dopamine rush. When they stop using, their brain may temporarily produce less dopamine, increasing the risk of a relapse.

Other mental health and neurological issues that may appear in people with low dopamine include:

Depression
ADHD and executive dysfunction
Dementia
Parkinson's disease
Too much dopamine may also damage the brain. Mental health researchers have long theorized that too much dopamine in the brain may lead to schizophrenia. The research on this point is mixed, and no single cause has been conclusively shown to trigger the condition. Because both too much and too little dopamine can be harmful, however, it is important not to self-medicate or self-diagnose a dopamine-related issue

CHAPTER 4

High Dopamine

High levels of dopamine and excessive dopamine activity in the brain can be debilitating.

High dopamine activity is linked to:

Anxiety
Excess energy or mania
Increased feelings of stress
High sex drive
Insomnia
Aggression
Hallucinations
Be sure to talk to your healthcare provider if you experience any of these symptoms, especially if you have some of the more

serious symptoms, such as hallucinations and aggression.

Academic Doping

Dopamine's impact on learning has led some high school and college students to take dopamine-boosting medications in the hopes of doing better on tests. This practice has not been proven to work and it is not recommended by healthcare providers because of the many potentially dangerous side effects.

Related Conditions

A wide array of medical conditions stem from problems with dopamine. Some are considered psychological, while others are classified as physiological, and still others as possibly a mixture of the two. Regardless of how the condition is categorized, it involves very real abnormalities in brain function.

Dopamine-related mental-health conditions include:

Addiction
Schizophrenia
Depression
Bipolar disorder
Attention-deficit/hyperactivity disorder
Obsessive-compulsive disorder
Binge-eating disorder
Movement disorders involving dopamine include:

Parkinson's disease and other parkinsonian syndromes
Huntington's disease
Restless legs syndrome
Some conditions classified as central sensitivity syndromes include dopamine dysregulation, including:

Fibromyalgia
Chronic fatigue syndrome
Addiction
Dopamine's role in reward and motivation is a key aspect of addiction. Whether it's

drugs, food, gambling, shopping, or sex, getting your "fix" gives your brain the good feeling dopamine creates. Your brain can crave that to an unhealthy degree, giving you the motivation to repeat the behavior that leads to the dopamine release.

 Overcoming Addiction
Technology and Social Media Addiction
A lot of media focus has been given to the idea that technology—especially smartphones and social media—is turning a lot of people into addicts. This is a controversial topic, but some experts say it's a real threat.

It may be that the constant rewards of social media (e.g., getting "likes" or "shares") sets up the same cycle of dopamine release and motivation to repeat the behavior that leads to addiction.

In 2019, the Journal of Behavioral Addictions published a study that

demonstrated parallels between people with excessive social media use and those with substance abuse and behavioral addictions.Help for Addiction.How to get higher dopamine levels safely
How to Increase Dopamine Levels Healthily
The status quo does not appeal to humans much. Whether we are looking for a new food, profession, or artistic endeavor, we desire for novel experiences and rewards. Dopamine is a brain neurotransmitter that drives these various activities. Identify it as the motivational chemical.

Dopamine does, however, have a negative side in the contemporary environment. Coffee, cocaine, and other very pleasurable substances may cause dopamine levels to become excessive. Additionally, modern tools like social networking and video games may have a similar impact on humans.
An An, the longest-living male giant panda in captivity in the world, has passed.

Peak dopamine levels may be followed by painful crashes, which are indicative of desires for additional thrills since our brains are designed to restore equilibrium. Repetitive indulging may cause tolerance, addiction, and eventually anxiety and sadness.

But by experiencing more wholesome dopamine highs, we may stop this negative cycle. This is the procedure.

Observe your compulsions.
The first stage is to become aware. keeping track of your daily routine to see if any of your habits are developing into harmful compulsions. Your smartphone may serve as a good illustration; stated in her 2021 book, Dopamine Nation, that cell phones give "digital dopamine 24/7." A recent study found that consumers check their phones for a third of the day.

addictive behavior is a continuum; even if a behavior doesn't fit the scientific definition of addiction, engaging in it excessively might nevertheless have a negative impact on happiness. Dopamine levels that are continually elevated may cause the brain to reduce the amount of dopamine receptors it has in order to achieve equilibrium, which would ultimately reduce motivation and all forms of pleasure.

describes a patient who developed an obsession with internet shopping in her book. New bundles eventually lost their appeal, and he racked up significant debts—yet he couldn't stop purchasing. recommended a full month without internet shopping in place of medications. He accepted her invitation to compete. Over time, his desire subsided, and he resumed experiencing "natural highs," such as the excitement associated with anticipating visiting friends.

asserts that not everyone needs 30 days. I've seen individuals readjust their reward circuits after a week of abstinence. On the other hand, not everyone can benefit from these breaks. People often need more forceful interventions, including medicine. However,"abstinence is the beginning point for many."

Long-term breaks from addictions may be effective in theory, according to Nora Volkow, director of the National Institute on Drug Abuse at the National Institutes of Health. However, further research is necessary to determine whether this strategy actually lessens undesirable behavior over the long term. According to Volkow, people are significantly more likely to succeed if they have social support networks and access to healthful activities that increase their dopamine and inspire them.

Get some beneficial pain
Healthy substitutions for unhealthy fixations make the most of the seesaw impact of dopamine. However, the opposite is also true: certain initially unpleasant events spur upswings in motivation and high mood—minus the fall. Dopamine peaks may lead to agonizing lows packed with desires. Hormesis is the term for the result. According to Robert Sapolsky, a Stanford scientist who wrote about dopamine in his 2017 book Behave, "well-timed deprivation may do wonders for pleasure."

taking cold showers as an example of hormesis. Though further studies are required, some data suggests that the body reacts to excruciatingly cold water by upregulating feel-good chemicals like dopamine. She describes them as "small natural pleasures without a significant comedown."

Camping vacations provide Kenneth Kishida, a neuroscientist at Wake Forest University who studies dopamine variations, hormesis. He was roughing it for many days in state parks, not glamping. This entails taking chilly baths, eating only occasionally, and sleeping in a little tent. It's incredibly challenging, but I always feel renewed when I return,
As we age, exercise has also been found to preserve dopamine receptors. Otherwise, they decline by roughly 10% every ten years.

Do not combine pleasures.

Just be cautious not to combine exercise too often with other stimulating activities like texting or playing loud music."we need some time when we're not activating our minds." "We cannot really understand pleasure until we have felt suffering." Wendy Suzuki, a neurologist at NYU who focuses on fitness, believes that music may be a powerful motivator. Most individuals won't find exercise enjoyable enough to do it often without music, according to her.

Volkow forbade the use of caffeine, another substance that individuals utilize to increase their performance. Her study demonstrates that it interferes with the brain's balancing function by impeding the removal of dopamine receptors in response to dopamine spikes. Energy drinks are often used by video gamers, which makes the game more alluring. To prevent obsessive gaming, Volkow advises being careful.

Try having your favorite combos less often rather than giving them up. This strategy is recommended by several experts based on the reward prediction error principle, which states that humans are strongly motivated by pleasant surprises. Every time we give ourselves the same really delightful combination, it becomes monotonous and predictable, which eventually lowers dopamine levels. However, if you indulge seldom, the novelty never wears off. No tolerance will develop.

Meditate
Meditation is another method for getting better dopamine surges. The Mindfulness Oriented Recovery Enhancement program, or MORE, was created by eminent professor Eric Garland of the University of Utah's College of Social Work. MORE has been

successful in treating opioid abuse, chronic pain, and emotional distress. According to a research that was published in JAMA Internal Medicine in February, almost twice as many persons who received normal psychotherapy benefitted from MORE, with 45% of participants being able to quit abusing opioids after nine months of follow-up. Daily meditation, deliberately appreciating sunsets, and other "natural pleasures" are encouraged by MORE. According to Garland, these activities increase dopamine levels without the spikes brought on by drugs and other addictions.

Teaching addicts how to deal with their emotions is another aspect of MORE. Garland asserts that "life contains both joy and sorrow." "Mindfulness enables us to thoroughly appreciate and accept both facets of human life."

Boost dopamine levels by entering flow states

"pain phobia" permeates our society. People often experience more happiness and greater contentment when they understand that some level of suffering in life is unavoidable. Flow states provide one example of this.

Rian Doris, co-founder of the Flow Research Collective, which investigates the biology of flow states, explains that people experience flow when they get so engrossed in a task that they lose track of time, which coincides with a modest but continuous dopamine spike. However, Doris asserts that in order to unleash flow, we must go outside of our comfort zones and through pain and hardship.

The Sweet Spot, a book on the usefulness of deliberate suffering, was written by

University of Toronto psychologist Paul Bloom. Paul Bloom claims that it is extremely difficult to engage in flow activities. "Watching Netflix while lounging on your couch is easy."

Take the example of wanting to write a memoir. Intensive, focused practice is necessary to master the trade, and according to Doris, "there's a strong need to distract with exciting tasks for quick dopamine releases."

But if you stick with it, you could finally be able to write in flow while producing chapters. Another instance is preparing for a significant race. Alexis participated in the New York City Marathon in November. She claims that running helps her to clear her mind. "It becomes easier the more you workout."

Moderation is important if dopamine is involved. Doris advised against spending too much time in flow, even at work."work has been drugged like everything else " for certain people. Take leisurely pauses. Social media and video gaming are fantastic outlets when used occasionally.

Bloom advises against seeing flow as a remedy for your Instagram addiction. It's simply another worthwhile endeavor in life. Even when they come with difficulty, meaningful activities are something that we all seek in addition to pleasure.

CHAPTER 5

Risky Behaviors Associated With Dopamine

You may have heard the saying that it's possible to get too much of a good thing. That idea is why dopamine can potentially become a problem for someone.
Let's look at what becoming dependent on the rush of dopamine can involve.

Sex Addiction
For one example, getting dependent on having sex can lead to sex addiction. Because it makes us feel good, we may seek it out in ways that are unsafe for us. This can involve having unprotected sex, having sex

with someone who is a stranger and might be dangerous, or not taking care of the responsibilities you have in life because you are busy pursuing sex.

Food-Related Disorders
Another example of risky behavior that can be based in the urge for dopamine is eating. On the one hand, we have to eat! We can't survive without it. And it's completely normal to want to eat foods that taste good to us.

However, eating can get out of control and become a food addiction, in which a person's relationship with food becomes more about eating to feel good than eating to stay alive.

Alcohol and Substance Use Disorders
A third example of how the quest for dopamine can lead to problems is with alcohol and recreational drugs.1 These

substances release dopamine in the most straightforward way of all, with drugs like cocaine directly flooding our brains with it.

Drug addiction and alcoholism can be life-threatening and can have terrible impacts on the lives of both the person with the addiction and everyone else they are close to.

In addition to the above, there are countless other dopamine-oriented activities that can lead to major problems and risky behaviors. They can be as big and life-altering as losing your financial savings due to gambling, or as temporary as exercising too much and obtaining a minor injury from overusing parts of your body.

Is Dopamine Addiction Possible?
It is not technically possible to get addicted to dopamine. It occurs naturally in our bodies, and we can't directly take it as a food

or drug. However, it is completely possible to get addicted to any activity that increases our dopamine levels.

Even though we aren't directly addicted to dopamine itself, we may be addicted to an activity because of the dopamine it releases in our brains.

Ways to Avoid Dopamine Dependence
Although it's important to perform activities that release dopamine, for the sake of feeling good regularly, it is also vital that you don't become dependent on that release.

It might be a shorter journey than you'd think to go from simply enjoying a pleasurable act on occasion and being hooked on it in a way that is harmful to your life (or the lives of others).

Below are some ideas to help you have a healthy relationship with dopamine and help avoid dependence.

Activity Boundaries
In order to avoid getting too much of a good thing, it can be helpful to have boundaries. For example, if you love to exercise but you find yourself getting hurt because you're overdoing it, set up your workout plan a week ahead of time.

Review your plan and consider confirming with a professional trainer that it is a moderate exercise plan and not one that risks you getting injured because it's too strenuous.

As far as how to set your boundaries, if you have a good memory you can simply think ahead and schedule out how long you'll spend with different activities or how much of them you'll do.

If you want to feel more accountable to yourself than that, or your memory isn't

great, use a journal to write down your boundaries or send an email to yourself.
Nerve-Calming Practices
Making sure you are getting enough relaxation in your day can help to combat the feeling that you need to perform dopamine-boosting activities more often than what is considered healthy.

Any self care practice can be calming to your nerves, as can very simple activities like deep breathing.

Conduct Activities Mindfully
Another great way to keep tabs on yourself and avoid getting too dependent on the release of dopamine is to make yourself more aware of what you do.

Mindfulness is the act of making a big point of paying attention in the moment, day to day, rather than functioning on autopilot all the time.

Before you set out to do something you enjoy that you feel you might be getting dependent on, check in with yourself.

Assess how you're feeling, what you're thinking, and any concerns you may have about your behavior. Then as you go along with that activity, continue checking in with yourself to make sure everything is feeling calm and not like you're getting too into the "high" of the act.

What to Do If Things Get Out of Control
Addiction is complex, and science is still uncovering why it affects some people more than others. Even though you can't be directly addicted to dopamine, you can get addicted to any activity that releases it.

If you've tried to mitigate your behavior and you haven't been successful, there are many professionals who can help you.

CHAPTER 6

How Addiction Is Diagnosed

You cannot get hooked to dopamine itself, but you may become addicted to behaviors that increase dopamine. Dopamine addiction, on the other hand, describes the issues that might arise when someone gets dependent on behaviors or drugs that increase the release of dopamine neurotransmitters.

The reward area of the brain is activated by positive experiences. Dopamine is released by the reward center in response to the circumstance. The brain is compelled to focus more intently on that particular activity or experience as a result of the production of this feel-good neurotransmitter. The second thing that occurs is that a person starts to remember the pleasure they had quite well. They then exert more effort to get those similar emotions once again by ingesting larger doses of particular drugs or partaking in addictive activities. A study that revealed regular use of addictive substances lowers the expression of dopamine receptors in the brain was published in the Annual Review of Psychology. As a result, a person becomes less interested in the other things they formerly found enjoyable in favor of consuming or thinking about the addictive substance.

Dopamine addiction is a fiction, to put it more exactly. Dopamine is not consumed in the same way as medications, food, or alcohol. However, engaging in activities that increase dopamine levels may lead to reliance and, eventually, addiction. Dopamine is after all a potent motivator that plays a significant part in the development of addiction.

Dopamine's reputation as a pleasure molecule stems from the widespread misconception that it induces euphoria, which is yet another dopamine myth. Although this neurotransmitter may help create euphoria and pleasure, it doesn't really cause such emotions. Dopamine links pleasant experiences with a strong desire to repeat that experience, reinforcing pleasurable actions and feelings.

According to research published in the Journal of Biomedical Science, the dopamine function controls learning behavior. In large part, addiction is also a taught habit. Dopamine neurons release in

bursts in response to certain behaviors or external stimuli, such as addictive substances, and this triggers a series of actions necessary for learning seeking.
Other Mental/Behavioral Illnesses
Several mental and behavioral illnesses are associated with dopamine dysregulation.

Schizophrenia
Dopamine plays a role in the psychiatric disorder schizophrenia. Other neurotransmitters, including GABA and glutamate, may be important, as well.

Older antipsychotic drugs work by blocking the action of dopamine in the brain, and the fact that they often alleviate symptoms of schizophrenia is strong evidence that dopamine is a culprit. However, some newer antipsychotics also alleviate schizophrenia symptoms without affecting dopamine.

Primary symptoms of schizophrenia include:

Psychosis (an altered perception of reality)
Delusions
Hallucinations
Disorganized speech and behavior
 How Schizophrenia Is Treated
Major Depressive Disorder (Clinical Depression)
Low activity dopamine has been implicated in some symptoms of major depression, including lack of interest and motivation.The neurotransmitters serotonin and norepinephrine also are believed to be involved in clinical depression, and antidepressant drugs usually target these two neurotransmitters rather than dopamine.

 How Depression Is Treated
Bipolar Disorder
Both high and low dopamine activity are theorized to be involved in bipolar disorder, providing a possible explanation of the two

phases of the illness: manic (extreme highs) and depressive (extreme lows).

Excess dopamine receptors and a hyperactive reward process network may underlie the manic phase of the condition. Meanwhile, decreases in levels of a substance called dopamine transporter may contribute to lower dopamine function and depression. The overall problem may be with neurotransmitter regulation, not simply highs or lows

Sometimes certain symptoms of bipolar disorder are treated with antipsychotics, which reduce dopamine activity.

 Management of Bipolar Disorder
Attention Deficit Hyperactivity Disorder (ADHD)
ADHD involves difficulties with attention, working memory, impulsivity, and hyperactive behavior. It's believed to involve low dopamine activity, possibly due to

certain genetic mutations that impact dopamine.

ADHD is often treated with stimulant or antidepressant medications that are theorized to either increase dopamine production in the brain or make more dopamine available to neurons by slowing down certain processes.

How ADHD Is Treated
Obsessive-Compulsive Disorder (OCD)
Dopamine, along with serotonin and glutamate, is believed to be dysregulated in the anxiety disorder OCD. In OCD, people develop obsessions (intrusive thoughts or images that trigger significant emotional distress) and compulsions (behaviors someone engages in to decrease the upsetting obsessions).

OCD may involve damped dopamine-receptor activity, and also increased dopamine activity in some areas of the brain.Most drug treatments of OCD involve antidepressants, which alter serotonin function but not dopamine.

Treatments for OCD
Binge-Eating Disorder (BED)
BED involves recurrent binging on large amounts of food very quickly, accompanied by feelings of a loss of control and experiences of shame, distress, or guilt. Dopamine dysregulation has been suggested as one possible biological explanation for this condition because it involves impulse control and the reward centers of the brain.

Certain medications that may impact dopamine function are sometimes used to treat BED.

Getting Help for Binge-Eating Disorder
Movement Disorders
Dopamine's role in the motor cortex of the brain is crucial for your muscles to make smooth, controlled movements. Inadequate

dopamine activity in this area is related to several conditions.

Parkinson's Disease
In Parkinson's disease, the neurons that create dopamine degenerate, leading to a chronic lack of dopamine.

Resulting symptoms include

Tremors
Stiffness
Difficulty walking
Balance problems
Speech and swallowing issues
Reduced facial expressions
Parkinson's is a progressive disease that gets worse over time. It's treated primarily by drugs that convert to dopamine in the body, increase dopamine levels, or mimic the effects of dopamine.

 Parkinson's Disease Treatment Options
Huntington's Disease

Huntington's disease is a progressive genetic disease that involves both motor and non-motor symptoms. It's caused by the deterioration of a brain region called the corpus striatum, which is an important part of the motor and reward systems.

Symptoms of Huntington's include:

Chorea (a type of uncontrollable movement)
Cognitive problems
Poor coordination
Mood swings
Problems talking and swallowing
Late in the disease, people can completely lose their ability to walk and talk. Huntington's can involve symptoms seen in psychiatric disorders tied to excess dopamine activity, including psychosis, aggression, and impulsivity. These symptoms are sometimes treated with atypical antipsychotics.

How to Treat Huntington's Disease

Restless Leg Syndrome (RLS)
RLS is a movement disorder that involves strange sensations and involuntary leg movements as you sleep or when you're in a relaxed state. The movements can keep you from getting enough deep sleep and leave you sleep-deprived, even after what would normally be adequate time in bed.

In people with RLS, a few areas of the brain are deficient in iron. In addition, abnormal levels of dopamine in the brain have also been noted. The relationship between low iron and dysregulated dopamine levels isn't yet understood.

Some research indicates that genetics and hormone abnormalities may also play a role.20 Many of the medications used to treat RLS are also used in the treatment of Parkinson's disease.

 RLS Treatment and Sleeping Better
Central Sensitivity Syndromes

Central sensitivity syndromes include a related group of conditions involving hypersensitivity of the central nervous system, which can include dysregulation of dopamine and other neurotransmitters. These conditions cause abnormal reactions to stimuli.

Fibromyalgia
Fibromyalgia can involve hypersensitivity to pain signals, light, noise, fragrances, temperature, and sometimes certain foods. Research suggests an association with low dopamine activity.21

Symptoms of fibromyalgia that may be related to dopamine deficiency include:

Muscle spasms
Cognitive dysfunction
Restless legs syndrome
Sleep problems
Anxiety
Depression

Mood swings

Swallowing difficulties

Fibromyalgia isn't typically treated with medications that directly impact dopamine, as treatment tends to focus more on serotonin and norepinephrine.

 Finding Relief From Fibromyalgia
Myalgic Encephalomyelitis (ME/CFS)
ME used to be called chronic fatigue syndrome (CFS), and the abbreviations are often combined as ME/CFS or CFS/ME.

It's a neuroinflammatory disease involving low activity of dopamine, serotonin, and norepinephrine. It features intense fatigue plus extreme sensitivity to exertion and environmental factors (e.g., noise, heat, chemicals).

Symptoms of ME/CFS that may be related to low dopamine activity include:

Cognitive dysfunction

Sleep problems
Anxiety
Depression
Mood swings
The treatment of ME/CFS is often aimed at neurotransmitters other than dopamine. However, the ADHD drug methylphenidate is sometimes prescribed off-label for this disease,and it does increase dopamine levels.

Low Dopamine in Fibromyalgia and ME/CFS

Dopamine-Affecting Medications

Several classes of drugs are used to treat conditions involving dopamine dysregulation.

Dopamine Agonists

Dopamine agonists boost dopamine levels or function and are used to treat Parkinson's disease and RLS.

Examples include:

Mirapex (pramipexole)
Requip (ropinirole)
Neupro (rotigotine patch)
Typical Antipsychotics
Typical antipsychotics lower dopamine activity in the brain by blocking a key dopamine receptor. They're used to treat schizophrenia and bipolar disorder.

Examples include:

Thorazine (chlorpromazine)
Navane (thiothixene)
Haldol (haloperidol)
Atypical Antipsychotics
Atypical antipsychotics are newer drugs that lower dopamine activity similarly to typical antipsychotics and also affect serotonin. They treat the same conditions as the older typicals, but with fewer side effects.

Examples include:

Abilify (aripiprazole)
Seroquel (quetiapine)
Clozaril (clozapine

Numerous circumstances can contribute to low dopamine levels. Low levels of dopamine will come from a reduction in the number of dopamine receptors in the brain caused by sleep deprivation. The morning will also make you feel sleepy and less aware.

Obesity has the same effect on dopamine receptors in the brain as sleep deprivation does.

Last but not least, stress can result in decreased dopamine levels. While a little bit of stress might be good for you, when it becomes a regular part of your life, it can significantly reduce your body's ability to produce dopamine.

CHAPTER 7

Natural ways to balance dopamine level

Dopamine Levels: Natural Remedies

Since dopamine is produced in the brain, it can be challenging to keep track of your levels, but there are natural ways to maintain a healthy amount. Concentrating on healthy behaviors is the greatest method to manage your dopamine levels.

Take purposeful breaks from dopamine-producing activities like sex, technology, and gambling if you find that you're overindulging in them. On the other hand, if you find that you're having difficulties focusing, lacking motivation, or feeling exhausted, you should try to make more dopamine.

eat nutrient-dense foods

According to Peterson, certain meals' nutrients reach the brain and aid in the synthesis of dopamine. Bananas in particular can help produce more dopamine, so eat enough of them.

Lean meats, fish, beans, and plant-based protein are all suggested by Peterson, as are meals high in omega-3 fatty acids including salmon, mackerel, oysters, ground flaxseed, chia seeds, and walnuts.

Regular exercise

Short walks, yoga, dancing in the kitchen, and at-home workouts can all assist to create healthy dopamine levels. Additionally, exercise enhances sleep patterns, which helps maintain stable dopamine levels.

"Engage in any enjoyable physical activity. Although forcing yourself to do something you detest solely for the purpose of exercising may have physical advantages, choosing movement that you enjoy will have a greater positive impact on your mental health "explains Peterson.

1.Enjoy the little things.
According to Peterson, doing something little that you like and consciously tying that act to a triumph or other nice event you observe signals to your brain that something amazing is happening and that you are in control of it.

This may be anything as straightforward as blowing bubbles, taking in the scent of coffee beans, listening to your favorite song, or seeing flowers in the garden. According to Peterson, doing this will increase the production of dopamine and provide you a sustained boost in mental wellness.Eat plenty of protein.

Amino acids, which are more compact building blocks, make up proteins.

All of the proteins in your body are made up of around 20 distinct amino acids. Some of these amino acids may be produced by your body, while the others must be obtained from diet.

Tyrosine, one amino acid, is essential for the creation of dopamine.

Tyrosine levels must be enough for your body to produce dopamine because tyrosine is converted to dopamine by internal enzymes.

Additionally, phenylalanine, an additional amino acid, may be used to create tyrosine.

Naturally occurring sources of tyrosine and phenylalanine include protein-rich meals including turkey, cattle, eggs, dairy, soy, and legumes.

Tyrosine and phenylalanine intake might raise dopamine levels in the brain, according to studies, which may encourage creative thinking and enhance memory.

On the other hand, dopamine levels may drop if phenylalanine and tyrosine are cut out of the diet.

While these studies indicate that intakes of these amino acids at very high or extremely low levels might affect dopamine levels, it is uncertain if fluctuations in protein consumption at typical levels would have a significant effect.

SYNOPSIS Tyrosine and phenylalanine, two amino acids that may both be found in diets high in protein, are used to make dopamine. Dopamine levels may be increased by very high intakes of certain amino acids.

2. Consume less saturated fats.

Saturated fats, including those found in animal fat, butter, full-fat dairy, palm oil, and coconut oil, may impair dopamine transmission in the brain when taken in extremely high quantities, according to some animal study.

These experiments have only been done on rats so far, but the findings are fascinating.

According to one research, rats who got half of their calories from saturated fat had less dopamine signaling in their reward centers than those that had the same number of calories from unsaturated fat.

It's interesting to note that these alterations took place in the absence of variations in blood sugar, hormones, weight, body fat, or body weight.

More study is required, but some experts speculate that diets rich in saturated fat may cause the body to become more inflammatory, changing how the dopamine system functions.

However, it is unclear if these effects are linked to dopamine levels. Several previous observational studies have shown a connection between excessive saturated fat consumption and impaired memory and thinking abilities in people.

SUMMARY
According to research on animals, diets rich in saturated fat may weaken the reward response by reducing dopamine transmission in the brain. It's unclear, however, if this holds true for people. More study is required.

3. Take in probiotics.
In recent years, researchers have uncovered a strong connection between the stomach and the brain.
In fact, the gut's abundance of nerve cells that generate a variety of neurotransmitter signaling molecules, such as dopamine, has earned it the nickname "second brain".
It's now known that some types of gut bacteria may also produce dopamine, which can affect your mood and behavior.

There is little research in this field. However, several studies demonstrate that certain bacterial strains may lessen the signs of anxiety and sadness in both people and animals when taken in sufficient amounts.

Although there is a strong connection between gut health, probiotics, and mood, it is still not fully understood.

Probiotics probably affect mood via increasing dopamine production, but further studies are required to assess the magnitude of the impact.

SYNOPSIS Probiotic supplements have been associated with better moods in both people and animals, but further study is required to pinpoint the precise function dopamine plays.

4.consuming velvet beans.
The precursor molecule to dopamine, L-dopa, is naturally present in high

concentrations in velvet beans, also known as Mucuna .

According to studies, eating these beans may naturally increase dopamine levels, particularly in those who have Parkinson's disease, a movement illness brought on by low dopamine levels.

According to a 1992 research on Parkinson's patients, eating 250 grams of cooked velvet beans dramatically increased dopamine levels and decreased symptoms for 1-2 hours following the meal.

Similar to this, various research on Mucuna supplements discovered that they may be less likely to cause adverse effects and even more effective and long-lasting than conventional Parkinson's disease drugs.

Remember that large quantities of velvet beans are poisonous. Be cautious to heed the dose instructions provided on the product packaging.

Another excellent source of L-dopa is fava beans. Eating naturally occurring dietary sources of L-dopa, such as fava beans or

Mucuna , may assist patients with dopamine deficiency illnesses, such as Parkinson's disease, recover dopamine level.

Despite the fact that these foods are natural sources of L-dopa, you should always speak with a doctor before changing your diet or supplement regimen.

SUMMARY L-dopa, a chemical that is a precursor to dopamine, may be found naturally in velvet beans. Studies indicate that they may increase dopamine levels as effectively as Parkinson's disease treatments.

5. Regularly work out

It is advised to exercise to increase endorphin levels and elevate mood.

Aerobic exercise may improve your mood after only 10 minutes, although the benefits are usually greatest after 20.

Animal studies indicate that exercise may increase dopamine levels in the brain, even though these benefits are likely not fully related to changes in dopamine levels.

Running on a treadmill boosts dopamine production in rats and modulates the amount of dopamine receptors in the brain's reward centers.

However, a 3-month human research indicated that practicing yoga for one hour, six days a week, dramatically raised dopamine levels.

People with Parkinson's disease, a disorder in which low dopamine levels impair the brain's capacity to govern bodily movements, may also benefit from regular aerobic exercise.

Intense exercise performed many times a week considerably improves motor function in persons with Parkinson's disease, according to multiple studies, raising the possibility that the dopamine system may be beneficial.

The present research is highly encouraging, but further study is required to establish the intensity, kind, and duration of exercise that best increases dopamine in people.

SUMMARY When done frequently, exercise may elevate mood and perhaps increase dopamine levels. To develop particular suggestions for raising dopamine levels, further study is required.

6. Get enough rest.
Dopamine is a brain chemical that produces emotions of alertness and awakeness when it is produced.
According to research on animals, dopamine levels naturally decrease in the evening when it's time to go to bed and are naturally produced in huge numbers in the morning when it's time to wake up.
But it seems that sleep deprivation throws off these biological cycles.

The amount of dopamine receptors in people's brains the morning after being forced to remain up all night is drastically decreased.

Reducing the sensitivity of the receptors should make it simpler to fall asleep, particularly after a night of sleeplessness, since dopamine promotes awakeness.

But having less dopamine often has additional undesirable effects, such diminished focus and sluggish coordination.

Getting consistent, high-quality sleep may help you feel more awake and high-functioning throughout the day and maintain the equilibrium of your dopamine levels.

The National Sleep Foundation advises individuals to obtain 7-9 hours of sleep each night and practice good sleep hygiene in order to maintain optimum health.

By going to bed and getting up at the same time every day, keeping your bedroom quiet, avoiding coffee in the evening, and just using your bed for sleeping, you may enhance your sleep hygiene.

SYNOPSIS Excessive sensations of tiredness might come from reduced dopamine sensitivity in the brain caused by sleep deprivation. The natural dopamine cycles in your body may be regulated by getting a good night's sleep.

7. Take in some music

A great technique to encourage dopamine release in your brain is by listening to music. According to a number of brain imaging studies, listening to music enhances activity in the brain's reward and pleasure centers, which are teeming with dopamine receptors. When respondents listened to chilling instrumental music, a 2011 research looking at the impact of music on dopamine discovered a 9% rise in brain dopamine levels.

Listening to music has also been demonstrated to assist persons with Parkinson's disease improve their fine motor coordination because music may increase dopamine levels.

SUMMARY
Dopamine levels may rise when you listen to your preferred choral and instrumental music.

8. Reflection
Clearing your mind, tuning in to yourself, and letting your thoughts drift by without judgment or attachment are all practices of meditation.
It may be performed while standing, sitting, or even while you're moving about, and consistent practice is linked to better mental and physical health.
According to recent findings, the elevated dopamine levels in the brain may be the cause of these advantages.

An hour of meditation resulted in a 65 percent boost in dopamine production compared to just lying still, according to a research involving 8 seasoned meditation instructors.

These adjustments are believed to aid meditators in maintaining a good outlook and maintaining motivation to stay in the meditative state for a longer period of time.

It's not known, however, whether these dopamine-booster effects only occur in seasoned meditators or also affect those who are new to the practice.

SUMMARY Meditation raises dopamine levels in the brains of seasoned practitioners, but it's not clear whether this impact also happens in novice meditators.

9. Obtain enough sunshine

People who experience seasonal affective disorder (SAD), which occurs when they do not receive enough sunlight during the winter, may experience sadness or depression.

It is generally known that exposure to sunlight may enhance levels of mood-enhancing neurotransmitters like dopamine and that periods of low solar exposure can decrease them.

The reward and movement areas of the brains of 68 healthy people were found to have the greatest density of dopamine receptors in those who had been exposed to the most sunshine over the preceding 30 days.

While receiving some sun may increase dopamine levels and elevate happiness, it's still crucial to follow safety precautions since too much sun exposure may be dangerous and even habit-forming.

According to one research, tanning sessions result in substantial increases in dopamine levels and a desire to repeat the practice in obsessive tanners who attended tanning booths at least twice per week for a year.

Moderation is key since excessive sun exposure may harm skin and raise the chance of developing skin cancer.

When ultraviolet radiation is greatest, which is often between 10 a.m. and 2 p.m., it's generally advised to restrict sun exposure during peak hours. It's also advised to use sunscreen anytime the UV index is over 3.

SUMMARY

Dopamine levels may rise after exposure to sunlight, however skin damage might result if sun exposure restrictions aren't followed.

10. Think about supplements

Iron, niacin, folate, and vitamin B6 are among the vitamins and minerals your body requires to produce dopamine.

You may struggle to produce enough dopamine to fulfill your body's demands if you are lacking in one or more of these nutrients.

You may find out whether you are deficient in any of these nutrients by blood tests. If so, you may take supplements as necessary to restore your levels.

In addition to healthy eating, a number of supplements have also been related to higher dopamine levels, although thus far, research has only been conducted on animals.

Magnesium, vitamin D, curcumin, oregano extract, and green tea are some of these nutrients. However, further human research is required.

Dopamine synthesis requires appropriate quantities of iron, niacin, folate, and vitamin B6. Some supplements may help increase dopamine levels, according to preliminary animal studies, but additional human study is required.

Dopamine is a crucial brain molecule that affects your mood as well as your motivation and emotions of pleasure. It also aids in controlling bodily motions.

Although levels are typically carefully controlled by the body, a few dietary and lifestyle adjustments may help you raise your levels naturally.

Your body can make enough dopamine if you eat a balanced diet with enough protein, vitamins, minerals, probiotics, and saturated fat in moderation.

Additionally crucial are lifestyle issues. Dopamine levels may be raised by getting adequate sleep, working out, listening to music, meditating, and spending time in the sun.

Overall, a healthy diet and lifestyle may significantly boost your body's natural synthesis of dopamine and support optimal brain function.

CHAPTER 8

Dopamine Detox/Dopamine Fasting

Delaying gratification
How to properly detox from dopamine
Purge of dopamine

Are you tired of how much time you waste online but you just can't stop?
Is it no longer enjoyable?
Despite knowing what to do, do you give in and choose to do something rewarding right away?
Do you find routine things that others like to be at all boring?
These are indications that a dopamine detox is necessary. But what precisely is dopamine detox?

The original dopamine detox seems to be a useful prescription for excellent online behavior, but we don't believe it will help you break your internet addiction or build decent surfing habits again. Simply said, it's a catchy statement that grabs our attention.

But there is a correct method to accomplish it, and this essay will discuss that.

In case you were wondering, we've compiled all of this information and more into a concise and useful dopamine detox guide.

Why would someone engage in a dopamine fast?

A dopamine fast may be beneficial for you for the following reasons:

You're tired with how you spend your time.

You are unable to resist stopping to surf.

You want to add excitement and enjoyment to routine activities (and not need to have your phone in your hand constantly just to feel engaged)

Have a healthy connection with your smartphone, the Internet, and the digital world overall. There are particular reasons for this, but the overall goal is the same.

Use the internet less

The objectives are:

to stop the repetitive cycle of obsessive actions, such as mindless online browsing or picking up your phone. For instance, YouTube video "rabbit holes"
realizing that just because we desire or want something, it doesn't always imply we'll like it after we've tried it. For instance, we could be overstating how satisfying it would be to play a certain game again. That is really simply our nostalgia at work.
allowing the brain to replenish its dopamine receptors so that routine activities regain their former sense of joy. E.g. You start a pastime because you once again like it.
The simplest method for beating addiction is as follows:

Success is the result of having the will to change, understanding addiction, breaking the obsessive cycle, building a better life, and improving emotional regulation.

In order to shift and end the obsessive cycle, a dopamine detox must be completed. This allows you space to develop a better life and, if you make an effort to do so, improve your ability to control your emotions.
What is the proper procedure for a dopamine detox?
How long should a dopamine detox take place?
typically 2 to 12 weeks. Our brains must gradually reorganize themselves.

The least amount of time needed to see results is two weeks, which is why our challenge was just 14 days long.

A suitable monthly challenge would last 30 days, which is long enough to see improvements. We advise choosing this course of action.

The usual length of time for Internet addiction treatment is 12 weeks (which is also close to popular 90 days or 100 days challenges). Although it is often lengthy enough to change your life, many individuals find it to be too intimidating.

1. Avoid activities that make you feel zombie-like.
Here is a general guideline for you: Cut out everything that sends you into zombie mode throughout the task.

Eliminate addictive diversion

When you browse, watch, or play for hours on end without truly enjoying it, yet are unable to quit or do anything useful, you are said to be in zombie mode. You engage in inexpensive dopamine activities for hours on end when you get stuck. The most frequent violators are:

Aggregators of content for social media (YouTube, Reddit, Hackernews)
Netflix binge-watching on Twitch Video game playing
Porn
Combination of all of the aforementioned, switching between them
You are aware of your specialty. You can catch yourself telling yourself that you don't need to stop doing these things because you can just learn to regulate yourself a little better and everything will be OK. You may give it a go. But often, this is a justification because

You wouldn't have the problem at all if you could control your actions. Additionally, these activities are often linked together, so even if YouTube is your primary concern, accessing social media frequently sends you there instead.

One of the objectives of the dopamine detox is to reestablish the capacity to control your behavior since it is very difficult to do so when your dopamine receptors are low.

Where can I get inspiration for this?
Your life may be in ruins. Or maybe you're doing well, but you still feel unfulfilled and like you're squandering a lot of time. Another indication might be that you have trouble stopping things like video games or YouTube. That can be an indication that you really need it.

It's crucial to have the desire to change.

If you're unsure whether to do this or not, consider these arguments against mindless browsing.

We won't lie to you; it could be painful for a time. Change can be difficult.

However:

It will be well worth the effort.
Making it is considerably simpler than you may imagine.
You may always revert to your earlier habits.

How to stop engaging in addictive behaviors
Remove distracting mobile applications, and block distracting websites in the browser... Take a few dramatic steps and remind your brain that you may return to Twitch when your dopamine detox is complete whenever you hear it telling you that you must watch it in the evening due to (insert crazy justification here).

What about tasks that you must do but which also encourage obsessive behavior, such as checking email?

Determine when throughout the day you are permitted to do this and for how long. For instance, you are only permitted to access your email for 15 minutes each at 10 a.m. and 4 p.m. (Pro tip: To do this, utilize our extension's Batch Rule functionality.)

As a reminder that you're attempting to change, you might also start a dopamine detox counter. It might be as easy as counting down from zero on a piece of paper how many days you've been following your new routine.

2. Take part in actual activities.
What to do during a dopamine detox is the next concern after eliminating addicting distractions.

You don't want to do anything except sit around.

Well, rushing toward something is simpler than running away from it.

You will probably relapse if you don't create a more fulfilling life without the Internet and if you don't work to address the root causes of obsessive technology usage. In little time at all, you'll return to your unhealthy behaviors.

What do we mean by a life that is more fulfilling?

You might do things that will make you feel good afterwards.

Dopamine detoxifying exercises:

speaking with others
Eating and cooking
taking a stroll
acquiring books
Journalling\sExercising
You'll see that these hobbies all move you away from screens, which is something they share in common with. Additionally, these

are all illustrations of what we mean by seeking high-quality leisure.

Describe in detail how you can spend your time more effectively. What are some simple things you might do if you start to feel a little bored?
Drawing? Journalling? Reading? Tidying?

Additionally, this is an excellent time to do some exploring. Enroll in a salsa dancing class, start an origami project, or pick up the flute. Make an interest that has previously been inactive.

Making a concrete list of these activities is beneficial. When you peek at a tangible list that is posted on your door or refrigerator throughout the day, it will serve as a reminder of productive ways to spend your time.

The activities listed above may not occupy the bulk of your spare time, so you should pick up any hobbies you abandoned or never began due to the Internet, such as playing musical instruments, sketching, etc.

learn new abilities
Develop new interests (remember those?)
The ideal situation is outside.
Find a neighborhood
You may decide on your addiction as well.

There are many options, so don't second-guess yourself and simply try things to see what could be enjoyable. Filling in the blanks in the following statement will help you discover potentially interesting hobbies: "I've always wanted to do ____________ but I never had the time or the chance." You will have the time if you detox off dopamine.

3. Only take in long-form stuff.
This is where the discussion becomes contentious since traditional "dopamine fasters" would see reading lengthy material as being dopamine-heavy. It would be

challenging to follow if you wanted to complete in 4–12 weeks, but we're here for the long haul.

Most individuals are unable to work continuously (although what we call work is often subjective). People attempt to make up for the time they waste in their leisure time by being more productive, but this is unrealistic.

We need rest periods and free time away from work.
Even if you begin to pursue more conscious leisure, you can become too exhausted to do so continuously.
Because thoughtless activities are what first led you into problems, you don't want to engage in them. Long-form material is the better option if you want to absorb high-quality stuff instead.
The best options are books and audiobooks. It's so much fun to play board games in person with friends. It's OK to watch one

movie without any interruptions. It's not to binge watch a Netflix series while going through your phone.

It's OK to merely listen to music. It's not if it runs in the background continuously.

We discussed the distinctions between viewing Netflix, television, and movies. The likelihood of compulsivity is reduced with long-form material.

High levels of dopaminergic activity have the following drawbacks:

You are motivated to act in ways that release the most dopamine by dopamine.

Here are several elements that contribute to dopamine-intensive behavior:

Time for stimulation
The behavior causes a dopamine increase.
intensity of the stimulus
Novelty

Of course, it's difficult to quantify this on an individual basis, but if you give it some thought, you can probably approximate it.

Drugs cause a significant increase and a crazily high level of excitement.

Playing video games may provide hours and hours of practically non stop excitement.

Porn is really unique and highly exciting.

The duration of stimulation is lengthy, but the intensity is not, as compared to longer-form entertainment like a movie.

How to prepare
As we previously said, carrying out a dopamine detox in this manner is definitely one of the greatest methods to rebuild a positive connection with technology.

Be aware that the first days may be difficult. You'll become bored. Fortunately, most patients get relief quite quickly.

Ordinary activities will begin to seem more enjoyable again after a few days.

Later on, you'll feel more in control, have more patience, and be less worried. Your ability to focus will progressively increase.

Other individuals have initial excitement and brimming enthusiasm, but after a few days, they kind of burn out and find it more challenging.

Before it becomes easier, be prepared for it to perhaps be challenging for a time.

Keep in mind that it will be worthwhile in the end. Once you've experienced it, you'll know what I mean.

Imagine how wonderful it would be to experience pleasure while engaging in everyday activities like wandering in nature, eating, or listening to music.

Just picture how pleasant it would be to be able to follow through on chores you said you'd complete.

Imagine how good it would feel to be able to quietly be with your thoughts instead of frantically rushing away to be diverted.

The Californian psychiatrist Dr. Cameron Sepah popularized dopamine detoxification, commonly referred to as dopamine fasting, after he published an essay titled "Dopamine Fasting" on LinkedIn and Medium in October 2019. Prior to this, the definition of dopamine fasting was mostly restricted to internet communities like Reddit.

According to him:

Dopamine Fasting is an evidence-based approach to control addictive behaviors by limiting them to certain times and practicing fasting from impulsively participating in them to recover behavioral flexibility.

The goal of Sepah's approach is to assist individuals in overcoming compulsive behaviors and gaining control over the continual barrage of negative stimuli in our life, including social media, online sales advertisements, pornography, and gambling promos. Contrary to other methods of dopamine detoxification that prevent using any technology, Sepah simply recommends that individuals limit their behavior if:
The actions upset people.
The behavior has a bad influence on your profession, relationships, and friendships. You've attempted to cut down on it without much success.

Dopamine fasting's main goal is to persuade us to accept unpleasant emotions like boredom or loneliness rather than turning to potentially addictive behaviors for an immediate, fleeting fix.

The gold standard in talking therapy, cognitive behavioral therapy (CBT), is the foundation of Sepah's approach. Additionally, he uses mindfulness practices to assist individuals in breaking bad behaviors, such as advising them to sit with their urges rather than acting on them right away. This behavior is widely documented in CBT and is referred to as "urge surfing."

Sepah lists six addictive behaviors in his widely read piece, including emotional eating, excessive internet use, gambling, shopping, pornography, and recreational drug use.

Despite its deceptive name, the dopamine fasting strategy aims to combat negative behaviors that dopamine reinforces rather than lowering dopamine levels. Dopamine is crucial to our health and everyday functioning, as we just discussed.

He asserts that we can achieve more rewarding, long-term goals and free ourselves from distressing or time-consuming compulsions by refusing the instant gratification these things offer.

I believe it to be a combination of CBT, mindfulness, and traditional behaviorism, while Sepah emphasizes that dopamine detoxification is distinct.

Regarding his conviction that we must have the ability to withstand the pain of boredom, the notion is not new; 400 years ago, the renowned French polymath Blaise Pascal proclaimed:

The incapacity of man to sit peacefully in a room by himself is the root of all of humanity's troubles.

9 798375 610269